The New Testament Teaching on the Role Relationship of Men and Women

The New Testament Teaching on the Role Relationship of Men and Women

George W. Knight III

BAKER BOOK HOUSE
Grand Rapids, Michigan

All Scripture quotations are from the New American Standard Bible unless otherwise noted. The NASB is copyrighted by the Lockman Foundation, 1960, 1962, 1963, 1968, 1971, 1972, and is used by permission.

The appendix, "Office in the New Testament," is reprinted from *Acts of the Reformed Ecumenical Synod: Australia 1972*, pp. 52–58, by permission of the Reformed Ecumenical Synod.

To
Virginia
and to our children
George and **Debbie**
Vann and **Diane**
Margaret
Jennie
and **Hugh**
with love

Contents

Preface

This book is an attempt to set forth the New Testament teaching concerning the relationship of men and women in the teaching and ruling offices and functions in the church, in public worship, and in the marriage and family relationship. I have chosen to speak of this relationship as a _role relationship_ where the question of authority, headship, or leadership is in view. Rather than attempt a formal definition here, I would refer the reader to the text of the book itself. I do regard this role relationship not as one that is assigned in the drama of life by our culture or society, but as one that is ordained by God for all cultures, societies, and times. This role relationship was established by God in the way He created man and woman in relation to one another and continues to manifest itself through the aspect of masculinity and femininity.

It should not be presumed that every relationship between or among men and women is a role relationship in which headship or authority is in question. There are many relationships in which this role question is not involved. This is true also with the people involved in the various other role relationships established in Scripture—parents and children, employers and employees, civil authorities and citizens, elders or church officers and the members of the church. When, for example, employers and employees join in concerted worship, this is not the sphere of employment and their roles are not then operative. At that moment they enjoy the commonality of the priesthood of believers and the equality of being joint-heirs. The same is true in one-on-one personal relationships where no specific role is in question. This is not to compartmentalize life, but to recognize that there are indeed appropriate and God-ordained spheres. To look at this from another vantage point, we may say that in the role relationships both factors are present simultaneously. For example, the husband is the head of his wife and at the same time they are equals and joint-heirs of the grace of life.

The preceding paragraph is intended simply to introduce a word of caution. Not every relationship that exists between man and woman is that particular role relationship of which the New Testament speaks. In other spheres men and women are not related as a husband and wife nor as elders and people but as those who are mutually dependent upon one another and relate to one another outside of a particular sphere of authority. Of course no role assigned by God is completely shed in the psychological and sociological dimensions of our lives. And the apostle urges that the questions of age and sex always be kept in mind even when the minister authoritatively admonishes the members of his congregation (cf. I Tim. 5:1–2). Even though older men and women are not the actual father and mother of Timothy the minister, he must appeal to them as a father or mother. Likewise he must appeal to younger women as sisters, in all purity. This passage shows that the questions of age and sex may never be completely disregarded even by the one exercising authority! To return to our caution, not every relationship between men and women is that of the structural and appropriate role relationship, but every relationship does have the overtone of one's maleness or femaleness.

This book focuses on the question of admitting women

to the teaching and ruling offices and functions of the church. This is the issue most debated and discussed. It must be clearly kept in mind that the author understands the New Testament to distinguish between these offices and functions and other functions and offices such as diaconal ones. The question of the marriage relationship is not dealt with in depth but only as an introduction and transition to the question of the teaching and ruling offices and functions. Therefore the section on marriage devoted to a positive exposition is exceedingly brief. Further exposition would have shifted the focus of the book. However, since the basis for the New Testament form of marriage, with its concept of the male head, and for the form of the teaching-ruling offices are the same and interlocked, it is imperative to approach the latter through the former.

Essentially two strands proceed side by side throughout the book: the first and most important is the exposition of Scriptural passages; the second is the answer to objections, particularly to the normativity of Scriptural teaching or to the historic exegesis or understanding of Scriptural passages.

In substance the book contains three major essays (much expanded and rearranged) and considerable additional material. The author would express appreciation to each of the publications for permission to utilize in rewritten form material that first appeared in their pages. The major part of the exposition of Scripture appeared in the *Journal of the Evangelical Theological Society* 18 (1975). The hermeneutical question of how one should interpret and apply the Scriptures is a major question, and it arises in this book in the first set of objections. If the New Testament speaks about slaves, kings, and women, why do we not treat that material in the same way? The answer to this question of interpretation was originally given in abbreviated form in *The Presbyterian Journal*, 15 September 1976. But there are many more questions about and objections to the historic and traditional exegesis, and the answer to the next set of objections reflects an interaction with Paul K. Jewett, Letha Scanzoni, and Nancy Hardesty that originally appeared in *Christianity Today*, 9 April 1976.

Appreciation is extended to the Reformed Ecumenical Synod for permission to reproduce the appendix.

I am particularly indebted to and appreciative of the good editorial services of Allan Fisher, a project editor of Baker Book House. Mrs. June Dare and Mrs. Robyn Crane, members of the secretarial staff of Covenant Theological Seminary, have done outstanding work in preparing the manuscript for publication. Mrs. Crane also prepared the indexes.

I offer this book with the prayer that faithfulness to the norm and spirit of God's Word will prevail in the church of Jesus Christ, for the glory of God and the good of all—men and women.

1

Introduction

The role relationship of women and men is one of the most discussed topics of our day, in evangelical circles as well as elsewhere. Two books claiming to be written from the evangelical perspective have aroused considerable interest: *All We're Meant to Be: A Biblical Approach to Women's Liberation*, by Letha Scanzoni and Nancy Hardesty;[1] and *Man as Male and Female: A Study in Sexual Relationships from a Theological Point of View*, by Paul K. Jewett.[2] These authors focus on the necessity for equality in the male-female relationship and presume that this rules out prescribed differences of function in the role relationship. The emphasis on equality and unity reiterated in the great redemptive passage of Galatians 3:28, these authors argue, means that there is to be no submission of women to men either in the marriage relationship or in the ruling-teaching functions in the church.

I disagree. I believe that equality and difference of role

---

1. Waco, Tex.: Word, 1974.
2. Grand Rapids: Eerdmans, 1975.

are not mutually exclusive but are indeed the two sides to the teaching of the Word of God on the subject. It is significant that the apostle Peter joins the two notes of equality and difference of roles in his treatment of the marriage relationship in I Peter 3:1–7. While Peter appeals to the husband to honor his wife as a "fellow-heir"—that is, as his equal—he also urges the husband to recognize his wife's femininity (as the "weaker vessel") and the wife to submit to her husband. Likewise, the apostle Paul writes of man and woman as one in Christ (Gal. 3:28) and also writes of the wife's submission to the headship of her husband (Eph. 5:22ff.; Col. 3:18–19). Equality and role differences are compatible.

This has been the church's understanding of New Testament teaching on the role relationships of citizens and civil authorities, of church members and those who rule over them, of children and parents, even at times of servants and masters, and of wives and husbands. With the exception of servants and masters (which relation the church understood as being regulated by the New Testament but not mandated by God), the church understood these role relationships to be established by God and governed by guidelines given by the Lord and His apostles. Included in these role relationships was that of male and female in marriage, one that evangelicals still recognize as normative.[3] For the same reasons, the church also has upheld a similar relationship between male and female in the ruling-teaching functions in the church; in particular, the passages of I Timothy 2:11–15, I Corinthians 14:33b(or 34)–38, and I Corinthians 11:1–16 have been understood as normative in this area.

Not unexpectedly, certain objections have been brought against this uniform New Testament and apostolic teaching. Full, free, and frank discussion of the matter is desirable; it will enable Christians to come to a clearer and more balanced understanding of the total Biblical teaching on this subject. But I am distressed that some who have writ-

---

3. Cf., for example, Harold Lindsell, *The World, the Flesh, and the Devil* (Washington, D.C.: Canon, 1973), pp. 135–36.

ten on the subject seem to abandon the inerrancy of Scripture and the authority of its teaching. Even some who claim to be evangelical Christians, to submit to the authority of God and His Word, are willing to appeal to the passages in Scripture that seem to support their position and to minimize other passages or declare them to be either wrong or only culturally relative and thus not normative, even when these passages themselves claim to be just the opposite. For example, Jewett, in his most candid and forthright way, says that Paul is wrong in his evaluation of the relationship of man and woman and in his appeal to and understanding of God's creation order in Genesis 1 and 2.[4] He and other evangelicals who hold similar views, when asked whether this is not a denial of the infallibility of the Scriptures, tend to reply—as Jewett did at a conference at Western Theological Seminary (Holland, Michigan)—that they believe in the full inspiration of the Scriptures and in its infallibility in reference to what it intends to teach concerning the area of "faith and life." But the sad and strange outcome of this qualification or limitation of infallibility is that its proponents end up denying what the apostles taught concerning one area of "faith and life." Such a view of infallibility denies even what it purports to save and keep. The unchanging Word becomes the changeable Word that must square with a changing culture which now has become the norm for man's life.

Others who depart from the church's longstanding view of Scriptural teaching on men and women would vigorously object that this is not a matter of one's view of the Bible, but of one's interpretation of the Bible—that is, this is a question of hermeneutics. Virginia R. Mollenkott and others allege that to interpret the Bible as normative in its teachings about man and woman we must also insist on slavery[5] and government by kings, about both of which

---

4. *Man as Male and Female*, pp. 134ff., 139, 145. Cf. also *Theology: News and Notes* (Fuller Seminary), special issue (1976): 20–22.

5. Cf., for example, Mollenkott's foreword in Jewett, *Man as Male and Female*, pp. 11f.

the apostles also give instruction. Truly the question of the Bible as God's unchanging Word in man's changing culture is a question not only of the inspiration and inerrancy of the Bible, but also of the interpretation and application of the Bible to man's changing culture. But a proper interpretation of the Bible, or truly Biblical principles of interpretation, will demonstrate that the teachings of the Bible display permanence, continuing relevance, and validity, even in the midst of a changing world and society. Therefore, the very questions raised will aid us in resolving the problem they thrust upon us and upon every thinking man and woman.

The church's traditional understanding of apostolic teaching concerning men and women has been challenged particularly in the area of church life and government. Vigorous discussions in Germany and the Scandinavian countries led to the majority of Lutherans in particular abandoning the earlier position.[6] Similar studies made in the United States resulted in a predominance of American Lutherans following the Europeans.[7] On a broader plane, most of the older American denominations have also altered their previous positions,[8] and the World Council of Churches has reported that a great number of its member churches have done the same.[9] The Permanent Judicial Commission of one American denomination ruled that an evangelical should not be ordained who said that his understanding of the

---

6. See the following: Peter Brunner, *The Ministry and the Ministry of Women* (St. Louis: Concordia, 1971); Krister Stendahl, *The Bible and the Role of Women* (Philadelphia: Fortress, 1966); and Fritz Zerbst, *The Office of Woman in the Church* (St. Louis: Concordia, 1955).

7. See the groundwork laid in Raymond Tiemeyer, *The Ordination of Women* (Minneapolis: Augsburg, 1970).

8. For example, the United Methodists, United Church of Christ, Disciples of Christ, etc. For a specific statement, see the *Book of Order of the United Presbyterian Church, U.S.A.*, chap. 8, sec. 2; and chap. 9, sec. 3.

9. Cf., for one example, Brigalia Bam, ed., *What Is Ordination Coming To?* (Geneva: World Council of Churches, 1971).

Scriptures would prohibit him from ordaining a woman to the teaching-ruling office.[10]

This ministerial candidate is not the only evangelical holding to this conviction. The Reformed Ecumenical Synod, when meeting in the Netherlands in 1968 and in Australia in 1972, reaffirmed as the teaching of Scripture the historic Christian understanding of the passages in question.[11] Also, studies coming from the dominant conservative wing of the Lutheran Church–Missouri Synod have reaffirmed the normative character of the passages in I Timothy and I Corinthians.[12] One might be tempted to generalize that while the more liberal wing of Protestantism has abandoned the historic Christian position, the more conservative wing has reaffirmed it, and that this reflects their respective views of the Bible, of its inspiration, inerrancy, and absolute authority. Avowed evangelicals, however, have opted against the historic Christian position. Scanzoni and Hardesty say that Paul's position on the role of women in church life is an expression of the culture of his day and is therefore not normative for ours.[13] Jewett says that Paul's position reflects his rabbinic perspective and is therefore not normative.[14] And, a majority of the invited participants in the Thanksgiving Workshop on Evangelical Social Concern voted to seek ordination of women to the

---

10. *Minutes of the General Assembly of the United Presbyterian Church in the United States of America, 1975*, pt. 1, pp. 52–54, 254–59. The assembly upheld the Commission, which declared, "it is the responsibility of our Church to deny ordination to one who has refused to ordain women." P. 258.

11. *Acts of the Reformed Ecumenical Synod: Amsterdam 1968*, p. 35; and *Acts of the Reformed Ecumenical Synod: Australia 1972*, pp. 58f. This last *Acts* includes two extensive reports of the study of Scripture which brought the Synod to that position. See the report of Advisory Committee VI, "Office in the New Testament," presented to the 1972 synod. Pp. 52–58. It is included as an appendix to this book.

12. See the last- and first-named books in note 6 and also David Scaer, "What Did Saint Paul Want?" *His* 33 (May 1973): 11ff.

13. *All We're Meant to Be.*

14. *Man as Male and Female.*

teaching-ruling offices of the church, although there was a large dissent.[15]

The subject, then, is a live one, even within evangelicalism, and deserves careful study. What follows is a presentation of the Biblical evidence first for submission and headship in marriage and then for submission and headship in the church, as well as answers to the major objections raised against these arguments. The role relationship of men and women in marriage and their role relationship in the church are founded on exactly the same principles, and the Biblical teaching on these two areas of life must stand or fall together.

---

15. See the reports in: *Christianity Today,* 20 December 1974, pp. 28f.; *Christian News,* 16 December 1974, pp. 1f. (a Religious News Service report).

2

Submission and Headship in Marriage

The Biblical Evidence

The Scripture itself provides us, in the momentous words of Galatians 3:28, with the framework within which any and all differences or role relationships must be seen and considered: "There is neither Jew nor Greek, there is neither slave nor free man, there is neither male nor female; for you are all one in Christ Jesus." Here the apostle, recognizing the differences between Jew and Greek (cf. I Cor. 9:19–21) and male and female, affirms that these are brought into one new being in Christ Jesus so that they are all one. With this word he removes any ethnic, national, racial, social, or sexual characteristic as determinative of one's spiritual standing in Jesus Christ. Faith in Christ and nothing else brings one into spiritual unity with Christ and into equality (cf. I Cor. 12) with all who are Christ's. The theological underpinning of this is the fact that all human beings are made in the image of God (cf. Acts 17:26) and that this image is renewed in the image of Jesus Christ (Col. 3:10–11; Rom. 8:29; II Cor. 3:18). Thus what is said in Galatians 3:28 is reiterated in Colossians 3:10–11, in relation to image renewal in Christ. We may therefore say that Paul faithfully reflects the Old Testament teaching of Genesis 1:27 that image quality is equally present in male and female. Thus both by creation and now also by the redemption that renews that created image quality, the unity and equality of male and female are most fundamentally affirmed.

So also the apostle Peter affirms this coequality and unity when he speaks of male and female, husband and wife, as joint-heirs (*sunklēronomois*) of the grace of life (I Peter 3:7). The aspect of Peter's treatment that is noteworthy for our question is that he affirms this spiritual equality in the midst of a passage which speaks of a distinct role relationship of wives and husbands, that is, of wives that they must be in subjection to their own husbands (3:1) and of husbands that they must give honor unto their wives as unto the "weaker vessel" (*asthenesterōi skeuei*, 3:7). The weaker-vessel terminology would seem to be Peter's way of stating the femininity of the woman, comparing the size and muscle strength of her body to that of a man's body, without intending to derogate the woman.[1] Peter has at once joined the equality and the difference as the two factors which must guide the role relationship. As we shall see later, Paul sees both equality (image-bearers) and difference (masculinity-femininity) to be equally the result of God's creative activity and order, and, therefore, both are germane to the question under consideration. He who can reflect Genesis 1:27 in terms of spiritual equality in Galatians 3:28 (and Col. 3:10–11) can also reflect Genesis 2:18–25 in speaking of wives being in subjection to their own husbands as their heads (Eph. 5:22–33; see especially vv. 22, 23, 31, 33). Both facets of creation come to their rightful expression. Spiritual equality may not be negated by sexual differences because we are both made and renewed in the image of God (Gal. 3:28; Col. 3:10–11). Nor does our spiritual equality as

---

1. See Gustav Stahlin, "*Asthenēs,*" in *Theological Dictionary of the New Testament,* ed. Gerhard Kittel and Gerhard Friedrich, trans. and ed. Geoffrey W. Bromiley, 9 vols. (Grand Rapids: Eerdmans, 1964–1974), 1:491.

joint-heirs of life remove our maleness and femaleness and the role relationship which that created difference brings to the relation of man and woman as instanced in marriage (I Peter 3:1–7; Eph. 5:22–33).

Objection Answered

If the New Testament requires wives to submit to their husbands, then it also sanctions slavery and requires government by kings. Opponents of the normative character of the New Testament teaching on the role relationship of men and women often point out that the apostles not only direct wives to submit to husbands but also require slaves to submit to masters and citizens to kings. And they add that instructions to wives and to slaves are often given in the very same context. Then they argue that if we accept Paul's teaching about wives submitting to husbands as universally valid and necessary, then we must also accept slavery and government by kings as universally valid and necessary.[2] Paul's teaching about wives, they conclude, must be culturally relative.[3]

We will deal with these three areas of slaves and masters, kings and civil government, and husbands and wives, and we will do so for several reasons. First, those who have advanced this objection to the traditional interpretation and application of the apostolic teaching concerning wives and husbands deserve a response. Second, these subjects touch upon important areas of life—that of one's work and freedom, one's civil government, and one's marriage relationship. These intrinsically merit our consideration. Third, since the apostles devoted considerable space to them, these items were important to the apostles and so are automatically important to us. Fourth, this objection to apostolic teaching concerning wives and husbands also has ramifications for apostolic teaching concerning children and par-

2. See, for example, Virginia R. Mollenkott, *Women, Men, and the Bible* (Nashville: Abingdon, 1977), pp. 92ff.

3. Paul K. Jewett, *Man as Male and Female* (Grand Rapids: Eerdmans, 1975), pp. 137ff.; Letha Scanzoni and Nancy Hardesty, *All We're Meant to Be* (Waco, Tex.: Word, 1974), pp. 91, 107, 202–5.

ents. The household regulations given by the apostles usually begin with the subject of wives and husbands and end with the subject of slaves and masters, but in between is the subject of children and parents. So far these opponents have been silent about whether or not the teaching concerning children and parents, like the teaching concerning other household relationships, is to be set aside, but their logic, which would have all items in the list of household regulations stand or fall together, would lead one to do just this. And finally, a proper interpretation of these three subjects, noting the similarities in and differences between the ways in which the Bible handles each, will provide us with specific principles of interpretation which will in turn help us properly to understand the Bible and apply it to our lives.

1. We turn first of all to the area of slaves and masters. Restricting ourselves to the New Testament, we find this subject dealt with directly and specifically in Ephesians 6:5–9; Colossians 3:22–25; I Timothy 6:1–2; I Peter 2:18ff.; and Philemon. It is clear that the first three passages instruct slaves to honor, obey, and serve their masters, and that Ephesians instructs masters to treat their slaves with goodness in reciprocity, to "do the same thing to them" and "give up threatening" (Eph. 6:9). Both slaves and masters are reminded that they have a Lord and Master in heaven whom they serve even in these activities and roles and that "there is no partiality with Him" (Eph. 6:9; cf. Col. 3:25). This is the essence of the motivation Paul uses in his instructions to slaves and masters.

Now the question for us and our day is: Does Paul's instruction for slaves and masters mean that the Scriptures regard this relationship as a God-ordained institution to be perpetuated? The answer with which we must respond, because of these very passages, is no. The apostle Paul instructs men in the situation in which they find themselves without implying that he as the spokesman for God desires to perpetuate this situation. We draw this conclusion from three considerations.

First, nothing in the passages dealing with slaves and masters indicates that the relationship is ordained by God.

Paul does not argue, as he does with parents and children and with husbands and wives, that these are God-ordained roles established by God. He only tells the slaves and masters how they should conduct themselves in the situation in which they find themselves, whether it is the best situation or not. (I think that Paul sowed the seed for the abolishment of the slave relationship in his remarks to Philemon concerning Onesimus; see verses 10, 12, 14, 15–17, and especially 21.)

Second, I Corinthians 7:20 demonstrates that Paul's approach to life is to direct men to live as Christians in whatever condition they are, neither ignoring that condition in a sinful world nor ranting against it: "Let each man remain in that condition in which he was called." Paul even applies this principle directly to slaves: "Were you called while a slave? Do not worry about it. . . ." (I Cor. 7:21). The apostle recognizes, however, that the slave might be freed, as is apparent in either interpretation of the rest of verse 21 but is especially clear in this translation: ". . . but if you are able also to become free, rather do that."[4] Verse 21, then, makes it clear that Paul can at the same time instruct slaves how to conduct themselves and recognize that their slavery and the institution itself can indeed come to an end. His principle is first and foremost to instruct men how to live in the socio-economic situation in which they find themselves. He is not establishing or perpetuating slavery at all, but rather telling slaves how to live in a Christian way. The beauty and power of this approach is that Christianity has something to say to men in this difficult situation, rather than simply saying that their situation is hopeless or that they should riot or adopt some other violent course. It is the Christianity of the God of love and mercy who through His apostles finds men and ministers to them in the situations in which they are living.

Third, Paul's approach to slavery is essentially the same

---

4. For an outstanding discussion see S. Scott Bartchy, *Mallon Chrēsai: First-Century Slavery and the Interpretation of I Corinthians 7:21*, Society of Biblical Literature Dissertation Series, no. 11 (Missoula, Mont.: The Society of Biblical Literature, 1973).

as Moses' approach to divorce. Jesus said, "Because of your hardness of heart, Moses permitted you to divorce your wives; but from the beginning it has not been this way" (Matt. 19:8). In my judgment, Jesus indicated that God, through Moses, regulated divorce because of the hardness of their hearts, not because He wanted them to practice divorce. In like manner God, through the apostles, regulated slavery.

This discussion has shown that God's Word is true and unchanging. It shows how slaves and masters should relate to one another wherever and whenever slavery exists. And since Paul addresses the question of work through or by means of the more specific situation of slavery, those principles concerning work, stripped of their unique slave-master nuances, are still valid for us today in the similar, albeit also different, employee-employer relationship.

2. Next is the realm of the state and its government. Again restricting ourselves to the New Testament, we find this question most directly dealt with in Romans 13:1–7, I Peter 2:13–17, and Titus 3:1–3. The point at issue here is that Peter speaks specifically of a king in I Peter 2:13, 17. And of course it would seem that the highest government official in view in the Pauline passages is also a king, not to mention our Lord's reference to Caesar.

But when Peter says "Submit yourselves for the Lord's sake . . . to a king as the one in authority, or to governors as sent by him" (I Peter 2:13) and ". . . honor the king" (I Peter 2:17), he is clearly enunciating a specific application of a general principle. Verse 13 begins, "Submit yourselves for the Lord's sake to every human institution. . . ." The principle is not that there must be kings and governors, but that Christians must submit to the human institution of government in whatever form or shape it may take and whoever the civil authorities may be (cf. Titus 3:1ff.)—so long as this allegiance does not conflict with their absolute allegiance to God. Paul demonstrates the same abiding principle when he states the truth in general terms, using the general phrase "governing authorities" rather than the word "kings": "Let every person be in subjection to the governing authorities. . . ." (Rom.

13:1). This understanding is undergirded when one recognizes that Romans 13:1 concludes with a general statement of principle without reference to kings: "For there is no authority except from God, and those which exist are established by God." The sum of the matter is that civil government is an institution ordained by God. The New Testament reference to kings, or even to governors for that matter, is simply a direct application of the principle to the situation that' obtained for the original recipients of Peter's first letter. Here we see that the institution of government is ordained by God for all places and every age, and that the form of that institution is whatever form God's providence allows to exist from place to place and from age to age. Again we see that God's Word is unchanging in the midst of man's changing culture.

3. Last is the area of the marriage relationship. What is the ground for the husband's headship and the wife's submission? Paul appeals persistently to the way God made man and woman and the way He made them to relate to one another. This is seen indirectly in Paul's quotation of Genesis 2:24 in Ephesians 5:31 and directly in both his appeal to the law in I Corinthians 14:34 and his expression of the law's substance in I Timothy 2:13-14 ("For it was Adam who was first created, and then Eve"). Paul's exposition of Genesis 2:21-24, found in I Corinthians 11:8-9, is: "For man does not originate from woman, but woman from man; for indeed man was not created for the woman's sake, but woman for the man's sake." Paul offers this exposition as the basis 'for his statement that "the man is the head of a woman."

This argument is based not on some cultural consideration that changes as man's culture changes, but on the most basic of considerations for human conduct—how God created man and woman in relation to one another. Just as Jesus appeals to God's creation activity to indicate God's will for permanence in marriage, so Paul, Christ's apostle, appeals to creation to indicate the relationship that husbands and wives should sustain to each other (cf. Matt. 19:4-6).

Some might suggest that the Bible, as in the case of

slavery, does not *require* marriage but only *regulates* it as an institutional phenomenon that exists in man's culture. Surely the word of our Lord Jesus concerning marriage is adequate refutation of this idea: "What therefore God has joined together, let no man separate" (Matt. 19:6). This is not an item like the relationship of slaves and masters which Christ and the apostles regulate but do not desire to continue. On the contrary, Christ desires to continue the very form of marriage.

Others might suggest that this subject of woman and man should be handled as the question of kings was handled. That is, marriage is permanent, but the identity of the head or the authority can change along with man's culture. When in man's culture kings rule, then Christian men and women should submit to kings; and when in man's culture the husband rules, then wives should submit to husbands. All the Bible wants to preserve is stability in government and marriage, and it is not concerned with *who* rules in each realm, according to this argument. The fallacy of this argument is that it overturns the very form which the apostles seek to establish and continue as a permanent element in marriage. The apostles do not argue just for some authority in marriage, but explicitly and particularly for man's authority and headship over woman and woman's submission to man (Eph. 5:22–33; Col. 3: 18–19; I Peter 3:1–7). For the basis of man's headship and woman's submission, the apostle Paul appeals to the analogy of God the Father's headship over Jesus Christ, His incarnate Son (I Cor. 11:3); to God's creative activity (creating woman *from* man) and its significance (I Cor. 11:8–9; see Gen. 2:18–24); and to the analogy of Christ's headship over the church and its submission to Him (Eph. 5:22–33). With full authority and with absolute and permanent reasons, Paul argues for the form of this relationship between man and woman. One would have to deny Paul's argument or his explanation and application of Genesis 2 to overturn the fact that this is the teaching of the apostles which they intended to be believed and obeyed.

The teaching of the Word of God concerning slaves and masters is true and unchanging for that relationship even though the Word of God itself recognizes that the relationship may completely pass away; the teaching of the Word of God concerning civil government is true and unchanging even though the Word of God recognizes itself that the form of civil government—e.g., kings—may change; the teaching of the Word of God concerning man and woman in marriage is true and unchanging because that relationship is established by God's creative activity. In this last relationship, Christians must oppose man's changing culture if and when it seeks to revise or overturn this standard of God. Notice carefully that the unchanging Word of God speaks authoritatively to the culture of man that God allows to pass away (slavery), to the culture of man that God allows man to appropriately change (civil government), and to the culture of man that God requires man to maintain (the form of authority and headship in marriage). It is imperative that we distinguish the areas of man's culture and not confuse them as some have done and are doing. We must always understand, believe, and apply God's unchanging Word in the way in which He directs us from within that Word itself. Only then does it continue to be the authoritative Word of God which stands over man's changing culture.

3

Submission and Headship
in the Church

The Biblical Evidence

When we focus on the question of the possible role relationships in the teaching-ruling functions in the church, it is appropriate to ask if that question is dealt with explicitly in the New Testament, and, if it is, to concentrate our attention on such didactic passages. This is basic to the proper handling of the Scriptures and the resolution of any question, and it will prevent us from drawing erroneous conclusions from passages which treat the subject only incidentally. In this case we have three passages: I Timothy 2:11–15, which most clearly gives both the apostle Paul's verdict and his reason for that verdict; I Corinthians 11:1–16, which explains the significance of this reason; and I Corinthians 14:33b–38, which presents the apostle's command and his reason for it in more general terms.

I Timothy 2:11–15. The setting for I Timothy 2:11–15 is a letter in which Paul instructs Timothy about the life of the church. Paul says explicitly that he is writing so that Timothy may "know how one ought to conduct himself in the household of God, which is the church of the living God, the pillar and support of the truth" (3:14–15). While the limits of this reference may extend to the whole letter, it certainly encompasses at least chapters 2 and 3. In chapter 2 Paul first writes about prayer, referring particularly to the responsibility of men. Then he turns to women and speaks of the need for modesty in dress, for a repudiation of ostentatiousness and a concentration instead on the adornment of good works (2:9–10).

After a general statement which requests women to learn in quietness and all subjection (*pasēi hypotagēi; hypotagē,* or subjection, is also the keynote found in the wife-husband relationship [Eph. 5; I Peter 3]), he then makes that aspect of subjection more explicit by a definite negative: "But I do not allow a woman to teach or exercise authority over a man, but to remain quiet" (v. 12). That which is prohibited is teaching *(didaskein)* and having dominion *(authentein).*[1] The prohibition is not that a woman may not teach anyone (cf. Titus 2:3–4) but that within the church she must not teach and have authority over a man *(andros).*

It has been suggested that this prohibition applies only to wives, not to women in general.[2] It is true that the two Greek words used here for *man* and *woman (anēr* and *gunē)* can designate not only man and woman in general but also husband and wife in particular.[3] However, there is no evidence in the larger context that the terms are meant to be restricted in the passage, or that they become more restricted in the verses under consideration. Contrariwise, the terms would seem to be meant more generally in verses

---

1. *Authentein* means to "have authority . . . over someone." Walter Bauer, William F. Arndt, and F. Wilbur Gingrich, *A Greek-English Lexicon of the New Testament and Other Early Christian Literature,* 4th ed. (Chicago: University of Chicago, 1957), p. 120. The word is a New Testament *hapax.* See James Hope Moulton and George Milligan, *The Vocabulary of the Greek Testament* (Grand Rapids: Eerdmans, n.d.), p. 91.

2. C. K. Barrett, *The Pastoral Epistles* (Oxford: Clarendon, 1963), p. 55.

3. See Bauer, Arndt, and Gingrich, *Greek-English Lexicon,* pp. 65–66, 167.

8–10 and, therefore, also in verses 11ff. Thus the prohibition of the apostle has to do with maleness and femaleness, not just with the married estate or relationship.

The reason for such a vigorous prohibition ("I do not allow," *epitrepō*)[4] follows immediately in verses 13 and 14: "For it was Adam who was first created, and then Eve. And it was not Adam who was deceived, but the woman being quite deceived, fell into transgression." The first statement is that the order in which God created man and woman (Adam and Eve) expresses and determines the relationship God intended and the order of authority. The one formed first is to have dominion, the one formed after and from him is to be in subjection. Paul develops this argument and its implications in I Corinthians 11, and we shall turn to that passage shortly. The second statement is related to the fall and the fact that Eve (woman) was beguiled. Paul does not expand and develop this argument, and we must be content with his brief statement of it. One may only conjecture that the apostle cites this foundational incident to indicate that when the roles established by God in creation were reversed by Eve, it manifestly had a disastrous effect. It is noteworthy that no cultural reason is given or even alluded to in this passage; Paul gives instead only the most basic, foundational reason, one which is always germane to men and women—namely, God's creation order and the dire consequences

---

4. The word *epitrepō* is used three times by the apostle Paul (I Cor. 14:34; 16:7; I Tim. 2:12). Two of the places (I Cor. 14:34 and I Tim. 2:12) refer to the same issue—women speaking authoritatively or teaching in the church. The other (I Cor. 16:7) refers to an action of the Lord. These three occurrences help determine the strength of the term's New Testament meaning, which has not been in doubt except for the present controversy and which is given by Bauer, Arndt, and Gingrich as "allow, permit." *Greek-English Lexicon*, p. 303. Its usage by Paul with reference to the Lord in I Corinthians 16:7 demonstrates the term's strong sense of absoluteness. That this is the sense in I Corinthians 14:34 is made evident when Paul says in verse 37 that "the things which I write to you [including verse 34] are the Lord's commandment." Since I Corinthians 14:34 and I Timothy 2:12 use the same word about essentially the same subject, we may with confidence regard the "I do not allow" of I Timothy 2:12 as an expression by Paul of that which he regards as "the Lord's commandment."

of reversing the roles, as evidenced in the fall. No more basic and binding reason could be cited. Paul thus follows the example of Jesus Christ who, when He dealt with the basic question of the permanence of the marriage relationship, cited the Father's creative action (cf. Matt. 19:3ff.).

I Corinthians 11:1–16. The reason Paul gives in I Timothy 2:13–14, is developed in I Corinthians 11:1–16. In I Corinthians 11 Paul discusses the freedom that the Corinthian women felt they had, to abandon the order which God has ordained and expresses in nature.[5] Paul argues that our freedom in Christ does not allow us to overturn this order and the particular expression of it in Corinth and the apostolic age. But he is careful to insist at the end of his argument that God Himself has, by means of long hair, provided the covering needed. So he ends: "... but if a woman has long hair, it is a glory to her. For her hair is given to her for a covering" (I Cor. 11:15). We thus have two things intertwined in this passage, the expression of the principle at stake in a particular practice and the natural provision, long hair, that God has given which expresses at all times the principle.

Paul begins his argument about the role relationship of men and women by placing it in the hierarchy of headships *(kephalē).*[6] "But I want you to understand that Christ is the head of every man, and the man is the head of a

---

5. Paul's use of the word *physis* in verse 14 and in effect the argument from nature in verse 15 accords with his use of the word elsewhere. Of the word's eleven appearances in the New Testament, nine are in Paul's letters (Rom. 1:26; 2:14, 27; 11:21, 24; I Cor. 11:14; Gal. 2:15; 4:8; Eph. 2:3). The usage in Romans 1 and 2 most closely parallels the usage here. In Romans, nature is God's natural order, and to oppose nature is to oppose God's order (1:26). In Romans 2:14 doing the things of the law by nature is showing the work of God who has written the work of the law on the heart.

6. *Kephalē* is used, "in the case of living beings, to denote superior rank. ... The divine influence on the world results in the series: God the *kephalē* of Christ, Christ the *kephalē* of the man, man the *kephalē* of the woman." Bauer, Arndt, and Gingrich, *Greek-English Lexicon,* p. 431. Cf. Heinrich Schlier, "*Kephalē,*" in *Theological Dic-*

woman, and God is the head of Christ" (v. 3). By doing so he establishes the propriety of headship by appealing to that of Christ to man and God to Christ, and at the same time has shown that such headship is not derogatory to one's person, being, or essence. He sandwiches the disputed relation (that of man and woman) between undisputed ones to set it in a proper framework.

It needs to be noted that Paul speaks not only of Christ as the head and authority of every man, but also of God as the head of Christ. The headship of God the Father in relation to the incarnate Christ in no way detracts from or is detrimental to Christ's person as incarnate deity. His full deity, His being of the same essence as the Father, is not at all denied, nor must His deity be affirmed in such a way that the Father's headship must be denied to maintain it. The headship of God in reference to Christ can be readily seen and affirmed with no threat to Christ's identity. This chain of subordination with its implications is apparently given to help answer the objection some bring to the headship of man in reference to woman. Just as Christ is not a second-class person or deity because the Father is His head, so the woman is not a second-class person or human being because man is her head.

The apostle brings his argument to a focus by contrasting the glory *(doxa)*, or reflection,[7] which the man and the woman each display. The man, he says, is the "glory of God," but the woman, the "glory of man" (v. 7). As verses 8ff. seem to indicate, this evaluation is based on the more immediate creation of Adam by God and the creation of Eve from and out of Adam. Thus, the man will reflect and be the glory of the one from whom she was created, namely, man.[8] The argument is now advanced in verses

---

tionary of the New Testament, ed. Gerhard Kittel and Gerhard Friedrich, trans. and ed. Geoffrey W. Bromiley, 9 vols. (Grand Rapids: Eerdmans, 1964–1974), 3:673–81, esp. pp. 679–80.

7. See Bauer, Arndt, and Gingrich, *Greek-English Lexicon,* p. 203.

8. "The same point emerges from v. 8f., where the being of woman as *doxa* . . . is explained by the fact that the origin and *raison d'etre* of woman are to be found in man. Hence, man is the image and reflection of God to the degree that in his created being he points

8–10 on the grounds of the order of creation of man and woman and the significance of this order for the headship of man in reference to woman. "For man does not originate from [ek] woman; but woman from [ex] man" (v. 8). The significance of this order, also referred to in I Timothy 2:13, is now stated in verse 9: ". . . for indeed man was not created for [dia] the woman's sake, but woman for [dia][9] the man's sake." Here the apostle cites the order of creation explicit in Genesis 2:18–25 and the reason for woman's creation—to be a help to man (v. 18)—to establish and define the divinely determined role relationship. To put it in a composite of words from Genesis and I Corinthians, man was not created to help and be the helper of woman, but woman was created to help and be the helper of man. This order is not based on the fall and the curse (see Gen. 3:16), but on the order of God's creation (contra Krister Stendahl and many others).[10] Paul concludes this section by saying that this order ought to be in evidence "because of the angels" (v. 10), apparently referring to the supernatural beings who desire to see God's order preserved and God's glory displayed.[11]

Lest Paul's argument for the role relationship be misunderstood, he quickly adds in verses 11 and 12, as Peter does in I Peter 3:7, the equality and natural interdependence of man and woman. These verses indicate that the order referred to in verses 8 and 9 does not glorify man but

directly to God as Creator. Woman is the reflection of man to the degree that in her created being she points to man. . . . In this relation of man and woman we are dealing with the very foundations of their creaturehood." Schlier, "Kephalē," p. 679.

9. Dia with the accusative means "because of, on account of, for the sake of." See Bauer, Arndt, and Gingrich, Greek-English Lexicon, p. 180; Albrecht Oepke, "Dia," in Theological Dictionary of the New Testament, 2:69; and the standard Greek grammars.

10. Cf., for example, Krister Stendahl, The Bible and the Role of Women (Philadelphia: Fortress, 1966), p. 29.

11. See F. F. Bruce, 1 and 2 Corinthians (London: Oliphants, 1971), p. 106 and the reference cited there. See also J. A. Fitzmyer, "A Feature of Qumran Angelology and the Angels of I Cor. 11:10," New Testament Studies 4 (1957–58): 48ff.

teaches that "all things originate from God" (v. 12). So the concept of mutual dependence in the Lord is added to give balance and prevent false glorying or misunderstanding, not to negate the previous argument. Here again the role relationship of man and woman and their mutual dependence can be correlated without one concept destroying the other.

Some have said that it is not man and woman that are here spoken of but only husband and wife.[12] Again this understanding is hardly likely. This is most clearly indicated by the fact that the relationship in view between the man and woman in verses 11 and 12 is not that of husband and wife, but of parent and child, which seems to imply that throughout the passage the words have been used in the more general sense of man and woman, not husband and wife. There are also other indications.[13] A

---

12. Cf., for example, the translation of I Corinthians 11:3 in the RSV—"husband." Note that the NEB and the NIV returned to the more general usage, "man."

13. Ralph H. Alexander gives these considerations for regarding the passage as referring to men and women in general rather than to husbands and wives in particular: "Crucial for the proper interpretation of our passage is the determination as to whether the terms are employed here to refer to husband and wife, or man and woman. The latter sense has been accepted for the following reasons: (1) This is the normal usage of the two terms. (2) *Anēr* is the more popular term employed to translate *ish* in the LXX, though *anthrōpos* is often employed as well. (3) Verse 3 qualifies *andros* with *pantos* ('every') which would tend to indicate all men, not just husbands. (4) The anarthrous *gunaikos* stresses the nature, character, or essence of a woman in verse 3. If 'wife' were meant, the article would be more appropriate in order to identify, or specify, *the* wife of the man. *Anēr* is definite when related to the woman in order to signify *the* head, as is true of all three authority relationships. (5) Verse 4 employs the word 'all' when speaking of *anēr* and verse 5 does the same with *gunē*. This inclusive adjective along with the participles for prophesying and praying would tend to indicate that men and women in general are involved, not just husbands and wives. What would unmarrieds do when they pray and prophesy? (6) Verses 7–11 are concerned with creation as a basis for the regulations given. This, in turn, would tend to stress men and women in general rather than just husbands and wives. Verses 11–12 speak of the mutual interdependence of the sexes in the process of procreation. If husband and

most striking one is that in verses 13–16 Paul appeals to nature, and what is true in or by nature applies not just to husbands and wives but to men and women in general.

Finally, it is imperative to take account of the fact, evident in most of the passages under consideration, that the apostle himself regards the teaching as not limited to the local situation; there is no other teaching or practice recognized by the apostles and all the churches: "But if one is inclined to be contentious, we have no other practice, nor have the churches of God" (v. 16).

I Corinthians 14:33b–38. We turn now to I Corinthians 14:33b(or 34)–38. These verses come in the midst of a chapter in which the apostle authoritatively regulates the use of spiritual gifts according to the norms "Let all things be done for edification" (v. 26) and ". . . let all things be done properly and in an orderly manner" (v. 40). He requires any man who speaks *(lalei)* in a tongue to keep silent *(sigatō,* v. 28) unless there is one to interpret, and then only two, or at the most three, may speak in turn. Likewise the prophets are to speak *(laleitōsan)* in turn, and if another is given a revelation, the first is to keep silent *(sigatō,* vv. 29–30). It is this section dealing with speaking and silence that provides the setting for Paul to speak about matters in regard to women, using the same two key words *(laleō* and *sigatō).* And just as the order of God, who is not a God of confusion but of peace (v. 33), must prevail for tongues speakers and prophets, so it must prevail for women.

The speaking prohibited to women in verse 34 and the silence demanded is to be interpreted by two factors. First, the speaking *(laleō)* must be, considering the light of the

wife were meant, these verses would be illogical, for the husband does not come into being through the wife nor is the wife the source of the husband. (7) Verses 13–16 argue from nature which would give greater support that man and woman in general is being discussed, rather than just husbands and wives." "An Exegetical Presentation on I Corinthians 11:2–16 and I Timothy 2:8–15" (typescript of unpublished paper presented at the Seminar on Women in the Ministry, Western Conservative Baptist Seminary, November 1976), pp. 5–6.

immediate context and previous usage, public communi-
cation (cf. vv. 27, 29). Second, the correlation of speaking and silence found here is paralleled in I Timothy 2:11–
14, where what is prohibited is women teaching men. Such
an understanding seems most appropriate for I Corinthians
14. Therefore, women are prohibited from speaking in
church because it would violate the role relationship between men and women that God has established. In the
event that the prohibition against speaking and teaching
in the church be circumvented by women who say that
they are only asking questions and learning, the apostle
points in verse 35 to another solution that clearly will not
violate the prohibition of verse 34.

Now we need to note the reasons for this prohibition.
The appeal is to the need for subjection (*hypotassesthōsan*,
v. 34), which would be violated by speaking. This subjection is taught by "the Law" (*ho nomos*, v. 34). It is most
likely that "the Law" refers to God's law, and to the same
passage in that law cited in I Timothy 2:11ff. and I Corinthians 11:1ff.—namely, the creation order described in
Genesis 2. The violation of the subjection taught in God's
law is what makes it shameful[14] (v. 35) for a woman to
speak in the church. The apostle stifles any rebuttal by
asking in verse 36: "Was it from you that the word of God
first went forth? Or has it come to you only?" With these
pointed and crisp questions Paul shows that the Corinthians must not suppose that they originated God's Word and
order, or that they alone have some word from God contrary to the understanding and practice of the apostle and
all the other churches.

Although it is true that the word *woman* used in I Corinthians 14 is particularly applied to wives in verse 35,
it must still be asked whether Paul intends the prohibition
to include married women alone and thus to exclude single
women. Considering the parallel passages—I Corinthians
11 and especially I Timothy 2—it seems more likely that
Paul does not intend to restrict the prohibition to married
women. He simply refers in verse 35 to the concrete ex-

---

14. *Aischron,* the same word used in I Corinthians 11:6.

ample of married women—which most of the women in the congregation were—to provide a guideline for other and different situations than that of the married relationship.

Let us set this section concerning women speaking or teaching in church in its context—a chapter on spiritual gifts. Apparently some then as now claimed that if a person has a spiritual gift, he can use it in the church without restriction; the gift is from the Spirit, and who can impose order on what God gives? The apostle argues that God is a God of peace and not of confusion, that He wants things done in a proper and orderly manner, and therefore that an unrestricted use of the gifts is contrary to God. In this chapter on spiritual gifts, the apostle also refutes the apparent assertion that unless women are allowed to speak and thus teach in church, the church may oppose God and His Spirit. He says that such an exercise of that spiritual gift is contrary to God's order of creation (cf. "the Law," that is, the Old Testament teaching of Genesis 2), and that no appeal to spiritual gifts or freedom can set this aside. Later he explains how women may use that gift in teaching women and children (Titus 2), but here he simply refutes an erroneous appeal to the Spirit and spiritual gifts.

Finally we need again to recognize the authority with which the apostle gives this teaching and the application of it to all the churches, not just to Corinth. In reference to the former, he self-consciously categorizes this teaching as the commandment of the Lord (". . . the things which I write to you are the Lord's commandment," v. 37). In reference to the latter, the apostle puts the teachings of this chapter in the most absolute and universal perspective. He asserts the principle that God is not a God of confusion but of peace (v. 33a), then adds, "as in all the churches of the saints" (v. 33b). Verse 33b might, instead of concluding the sentence that begins in verse 31, begin verse 34. But whether it belongs grammatically to verses 31–33a or to verse 34, the lesson is clear that the teaching of the chapter as a whole and the teaching concerning women in particular apply to all the churches.

We conclude from our survey of these three key passages that the apostle Paul laid down a universally normative regulation which prohibits women from ruling and teaching men in the church. These passages are not illustrations but commands; these commands are grounded not in time-bound, historically and culturally relative arguments that apply only to Paul's day and age, but in the way God created man and woman to relate to each other as male and female.

This creation order and its correlatives of headship and subjection appear in each passage, just as this order and its correlatives provide the one and only foundation for the role relationship in marriage. To dismiss the role relationship in the church's teaching-ruling function as simply cultural would carry with it the dismissal of the analogous role relationship in marriage as also cultural, because they are based on the same principle. Letha Scanzoni and Nancy Hardesty do just that,[15] and so does Paul K. Jewett.[16] Likewise, if one preserves the role relationship in marriage because of the creation order, one also must preserve the role relationship in the church's teaching-ruling function, because it is based on that same creation order.

The fact that "there is neither male nor female, for you are all one in Christ Jesus" (Gal. 3:28) does not deny the teaching of I Timothy 2 and I Corinthians 14, just as it does not deny man's maleness and woman's femaleness, nor annul their relationship in the family (cf. Eph. 5:22ff.).

The exclusion of women from the teaching and ruling office and functions of the church in I Timothy 2:11–15 and I Corinthians 14:33b–37 must not be construed as all the New Testament evidence on the role of women in the church, even though it is very specific. Several passages indicate that women are involved in diaconal tasks and also

---

15. Compare the two chapters "Love, Honor and _____?" and "Living in Partnership" in *All We're Meant to Be* (Waco, Tex.: Word, 1974), pp. 88–117. Also see the term *equalitarian marriage* on p. 118 and elsewhere.

16. *Man as Male and Female* (Grand Rapids: Eerdmans, 1975), pp. 137–41 ("Female Subordination and the Bond of Marriage").

appropriate teaching situations. A sampling of these activities may be seen in the following: older widows are enrolled by the church (I Tim. 5:9–16); older women are called upon to teach and train younger women concerning their responsibilities to their husbands and children (Titus 2:3–5); women (or wives, *gunaikas*) are referred to in the midst of the description of deacons (I Tim. 3:11); Phoebe is designated "a servant [*diakonon*] of the church which is at Cenchrea" (Rom. 16:1); Paul refers in I Corinthians to women praying or prophesying (11:5); and Priscilla and Aquila, that inseparable husband-and-wife team, in a discreet and private meeting expound unto Apollos "the way of God more accurately" (Acts 18:26).

Therefore, in considering the ministry of men and women in the church, these three Biblical truths must be held in correlation: (1) Men and women equally bear God's image: "... there is neither male nor female; for you are all one in Christ Jesus" (Gal. 3:28). Therefore, men and women are, in and before Christ, equal. (2) Men and women manifest in their sexuality a difference created and ordered by God. By this creative order women are to be subject to men in the church and are therefore excluded from the ruling-teaching office and functions (I Tim. 2:11–15; I Cor. 14:33b–37; cf. I Tim. 3:4–5), which men alone are to fill. And (3) women have a function to fulfill in the diaconal task of the church and in the teaching of women and children (cf., for example, I Tim. 3:11; 5:9ff.; Titus 2:3–4; Rom. 16:1).

Objections Answered

Several objections have been raised against the traditional interpretation of I Timothy 2:11–15 and I Corinthians 11:1–16, and to these we now turn.

First, it is said that the statement of Paul in I Timothy 2:13—"For it was Adam who was first created, and then Eve"—is not significant for the role relationship of men and women. Scanzoni and Hardesty say, "If beings created first are to have precedence, then the animals are clearly our betters."[17] The point of Paul's statement, however, is not merely that of chronology but that of derivation and relationship, as his fuller handling of the Old Testament episode in I Corinthians 11:8–9 shows. The recognition of this point removes the objection of Scanzoni and Hardesty because mankind in general, or man and woman in particular, are not made from the animals. Nor is man derived from the dust of the ground as if shaped or fashioned from a living entity (contra Paul K. Jewett). The Old Testament narrative says, ". . . The LORD God fashioned [built] into a woman the rib which He had taken from the man. . . ." (Gen. 2:22). We see that Paul is concerned with origin, not with mere chronology, when we read the exegetical language of I Corinthians 11:8–9: "For man does not originate from woman, but woman from man; for indeed man was not created for the woman's sake, but woman for the man's sake."

The second objection is Jewett's argument that Paul's exegesis of Genesis 2:18ff. in I Corinthians 11:1–16 is inaccurate. When Paul sees in Genesis 2 an order of authority between the man and woman, says Jewett, Paul is exhibiting not what Genesis says or implies but a remnant of his rabbinic thinking.[18]

This matter of the way in which woman is made out of man is highly significant for the relationship of man and woman, as seen not only in the Pauline texts but also in the text of Genesis itself: "And the man said, 'This is now bone of my bones, and flesh of my flesh; she shall be called Woman, because she was taken out of Man'" (Gen. 2:23). In addition the next verse says: "For this cause a man shall leave his father and his mother, and shall cleave to his wife; and they shall become one flesh." Not only for Paul but also for Adam and Moses—as well as for God, who created woman in such a way and evoked the responses and principial applications—the created order and

17. *All We're Meant to Be*, p. 28; cf. also Paul K. Jewett, *Man as Male and Female*, pp. 126–27.

18. *Man as Male and Female*, p. 119. (Read this in the context of pp. 111–19.)

relationship is a most important factor in how man regards woman, how woman regards man, and how both regard their relationship to each other. The relationship of woman to man, as well as the cohumanity, comes through eloquently in the play on words in Gen. 2:23: "... she shall be called Woman [*ishah*], because she was taken out of Man [*ish*]."

> The woman is created for him out of his very being and the man names his new companion "woman." We see here the difference in function between man and woman. In hebrew thought name-giving is "the prerogative of a superior" (J. A. Motyer, *New Bible Dictionary*). God exercises this prerogative in Genesis 1, giving names to the things He has created. Man shares in this when he names the animals over whom he has been given dominion by God. So when God brings the woman to the man and he gives her her name he is demonstrating his God-given headship and responsibility. Yet in that very act the oneness and harmony that should exist between men and women is also illustrated. To quote again from Motyer, "When the name-giver places his own name upon the person named, the giving of the name signifies the joining of two hitherto separate persons in the closest unity." Adam's name in hebrew is "*ish*" and he called the woman "*ishah*," which is the feminine form of his own name.[19]

God's creation of woman from man provides the basis for woman and man becoming one flesh in marriage: "For this cause a man ... shall cleave to his wife; and they shall become one flesh" (v. 24).

It is prejudicial to assert that this activity should not provide, as Paul says it does, a basis for the relationship of men and women, for when the episode occurred and then when it was first recorded—under the inspiration of God's Spirit—its theological significance was vigorously af-

---

19. Bob Key and Daphne Key, *Adam, Eve, and Equality* (Leicester: Universities and Colleges Christian Fellowship, 1976), p. 7. The article cited in this quotation is "Name," in *The New Bible Dictionary*, ed. J. D. Douglas (Grand Rapids: Eerdmans, 1962), pp. 861–64. Motyer also says, "When a superior thus exercised his authority, the giving of the name signified the appointment of the person named to some specific position, function, or relationship." P. 862.

firmed. What Paul says in I Corinthians 11:8–9, is quite evidently the fact of the matter. Verse 8 affirms that man was not created out of or from woman, but woman out of or from man. Similarly verse 9 affirms that man was not created for (to be a helper of) woman, but woman for man. This furnishes the Scriptural basis for Paul's affirmation in verse 3 that the man is the head of the woman. He is saying in effect that if one human being is created to be the helper of another human being, the one who receives such a helper has a certain authority over the helper. It is said in opposition to this that because sometimes in the Old Testament God is called man's "helper" (the same Hebrew word is used of God that is used of woman), this argument cannot be valid. Cannot a word, however, have a different nuance when applied to God than it does when applied to humans? Certainly a different nuance or connotation of a word does not nullify the apostolic exegesis and application.

Furthermore, contrary to Jewett's argument that Paul's exegesis is inaccurate is this fact: the order of authority Paul discerns in Genesis 2 is presumed in Genesis 3, lying behind the judgment of God on man's sin. Genesis 3 presumes the reality of childbearing (Gen. 1:28), in which the woman will now experience the effects of the fall and sin (3:16). It presumes the reality of work (Gen. 1:28; 2:15), in which the man will now experience the effects of the fall and sin (3:17ff.). And it presumes the reality of the role relationship between wife and husband established by God's creation order in Genesis 2:18ff., a relationship which will now experience the effects of the fall and sin (3:16). "He shall rule over you" expresses the effects of sin corrupting the relationship of husband (the head) and wife. Just as childbearing and work were established before the fall and corrupted by it, so this relationship existed before the fall and was corrupted by it. Neither childbearing, nor work, nor the role relationship of wife and husband is being introduced in Genesis 3; all are previously existing realities that have been affected by the fall. If Genesis 3 can so readily presume that an order of authority between man and woman has been established in Genesis 2, surely it is erroneous to say that Genesis 2 does not and cannot teach what Paul says it does.

The third objection is that the role relationship of man and woman in marriage and the church is based solely upon the effects of sin and the fall (e.g., Gen. 3:16). Then it is said that just as we try to alleviate the effects of sin on childbirth with anesthesia and the effects of sin on work with air-conditioned tractors, so we should alleviate the effects of sin on the man-woman relationship by eliminating the headship of man. I have two points to make in response to this argument.

First, I agree that we should seek to relieve the effects of the fall and sin in all three of those areas. But we should do so not by eliminating childbirth, work, and the role relationship of man and woman, but by alleviating that which corrupts these three entities. With respect to the latter, the apostles urge husbands to love, honor, and not be bitter to their wives; they do not urge them to cease being the head of their households (cf. Eph. 5:22ff.; I Peter 3:1ff.; Col. 3:18–19). The removal of a husband's oppressive rule over his wife is not the removal of his headship over her or of their role relationship to each other; it is the removal, through love, of the effects of sin on the role relationship.

Second, the Bible never builds its case for the role relationship of men and women in marriage upon the effects of sin manifested in Genesis 3:16. The apostle Paul appeals to the prefall creation order as normative. (See Eph. 5:31; I Cor. 11:8–9; 14:34; I Tim. 2:13–14; the "law" referred to or quoted in these places is Genesis 2, not Genesis 3.) It is true that in I Timothy 2:14 Paul also refers to the fall after citing the creation order, but he does this to show the dire consequences of reversing the creation order on this most historic and significant occasion. God's creation order for men and women, not the fallen order, is normative for the New Testament.

The fourth objection to which we must respond is this: Paul refers in I Corinthians 11:5 to women praying and prophesying in the church. We must conclude, these objectors say, either that Paul here contradicts his injunctions to women to keep silent in church (I Cor. 14:34; I Tim. 2:11–12),[20] or that I Corinthians 11:5 must govern our interpretation of I Corinthians 14:34 and I Timothy 2:11–12.[21] But the latter two passages are clearly the didactic passages on the subject, while I Corinthians 11 only mentions the subject incidentally. Therefore, our interpretation of I Corinthians 14 and I Timothy 2 ought to govern our interpretation of I Corinthians 11, not vice versa. It also is appropriate to assume that the great apostle Paul does not contradict himself in the same letter and only a few chapters apart.

Several reasonable ways to integrate these passages have been proposed: (1) The praying and prophesying mentioned in I Corinthians 11 did not occur in the church.[22] Some would add that in I Timothy 2 Paul limits to men the activity of praying in the church.[23] (2) The praying and prophesying mentioned in I Corinthians 11 occurred in the church, but by mentioning the practice, Paul does not condone it.[24] He refers to the practice in order to get at

20. Stendahl, *The Role of Women*, p. 35. Eduard Schweizer says that the verses in question in I Corinthians 14 are a later interpolation and that they are contradicted by I Corinthians 11:5. "The Service of Worship: An Exposition of I Corinthians 14," *Interpretation* 13 (1959): 400ff. Although there is a slight textual problem, it is a matter not of the verses (34–35) being interpolated into the text but of their being in the proper place. Kurt Aland et al. in their textual apparatus enumerate the very strong textual witnesses to these verses belonging in the usually acknowledged position, giving this textual reading a B-level evaluation. *The Greek New Testament*, 3rd ed. (London: United Bible Societies, 1975), p. 611. For the basis of their judgment see Bruce M. Metzger, ed., *A Textual Commentary on the Greek New Testament* (London: United Bible Societies, 1971), p. 565.

21. For example, Irene M. Robbins, "St. Paul and the Ministry of Women," *Expository Times* 44 (1935): 196.

22. For example, Charles Hodge, *An Exposition of the First Epistle to the Corinthians* (New York: Carter, 1857), p. 305.

23. For example, Charles C. Ryrie, *The Place of Women in the Church* (New York: Macmillan, 1958), p. 76.

24. For a possible example, see Archibald Robertson and Alfred Plummer, *I Corinthians*, 2nd ed. (Edinburgh: Clark, 1914), pp. 324–25.

the issue with which he is dealing in chapter 11; he returns to the practice in chapter 14 and forbids women from praying and prophesying in the church.[25] Paul deals with the practice of eating meat in an idol's temple in an analogous way: in I Corinthians 8:10 he mentions the practice with seeming approval, but in I Corinthians 10:20–22 he appears to forbid it.[26] And (3) women may pray and prophesy[27] in the church because these activities are expressly allowed in I Corinthians 11.[28] The writer regards this third solution as the correct one. If this is correct, then it must be recognized that the apostle regards praying and prophesying on the one hand and speaking which involves teaching (cf. again I Cor. 14:34 and I Tim. 2:12) on the other hand as distinguishable and different activities. Praying publicly in the midst of others does not imply or involve any authority or headship over others. Likewise prophesying, an activity in which the one prophesying is essentially a passive instrument through which God communicates, does not necessarily imply or involve authority or headship over others (compare, if we may be permitted a hopefully inoffensive note of humor, Balaam's ass [Num. 22:22ff.]). What I Corinthians 14 and I Timothy 2 forbid, then, is authoritative speaking, teaching, and ruling. As is apparent, all three solutions preserve the didactic element in I Corinthians 14 and I Timothy 2 and are consistent with the interpretation of these passages that we have already put forth.

---

25. R. St. John Parry, *The First Epistle of Paul the Apostle to the Corinthians* (Cambridge: University, 1926), pp. 210–11.

26. Hodge, *First Corinthians*, p. 148.

27. I am persuaded by a study of prophecy in the New Testament (expressed by the terms *prophēteia, prophēteuō,* and *prophētēs*) that this activity is the result of God's Spirit acting in and through a person to produce a revelation and that this is intrinsically different from what the New Testament means by teaching and preaching. Although this conclusion might affect one's choice between the three solutions being offered, it will remain true apart from one's choice.

28. J. B. Hurley, "Did Paul Require Veils or the Silence of Women? A Consideration of I Cor. 11:2–16 and I Cor. 14:33b–36." *Westminster Theological Journal* 35 (1973): 203.

A fifth and final objection is that to affirm the traditional interpretation of the passages discussed in this chapter is to exclude or rule out women and their gifts from service in the life of the church. Such an erroneous deduction must be repudiated, on the basis of clear Biblical teaching, in both thought and practice.

Although the New Testament teaching about marriage is presented in terms of man as the head over his wife and family, no one deduces from this truth that the wife is not involved in a vital and real way, performing many exceedingly important and necessary functions, in the marriage and the family! Her gifts and graces have free range except when and where they impinge upon the headship of her husband. The same is true in the church. The exclusion of women from the ruling and teaching offices and functions in the church does not mean that woman has no place of service in the church. The teaching and ruling offices and functions are not the only gifts, functions, or services in the church. Just as in marriage and the family, so also in the church the activities and functions of women are necessary and important. No part of the body of Christ (especially men, in this case) may say of another part "I have no need of you" (I Cor. 12:21). And no part of the body of Christ (especially women, in this case) may say that because they are not occupying the office or performing the function of a leader, they are not a significant part of the body (cf. I Cor. 12:14–20). The truth of God through the apostle Paul is exceedingly important in our context: "But now God has placed the members, each one of them, in the body, just as He desired" (I Cor. 12:18).

The New Testament tells of women being involved in the ministry and life of the church in various ways, but always in ways other than the teaching-ruling offices and functions. References to women granting Jesus assistance in His ministry and to His interaction with them are well known and need no documentation. It is certainly noteworthy that women were present at the cross and empty tomb and that women were the first to announce the resurrection. A similar type of involvement and assistance to this is in view when the apostle Paul designates certain women as those "who have shared my struggle in the cause of the gospel" and as "fellow-workers" (Phil. 4:3). In Titus 2:3ff. Paul urges the older women to teach, within the church, the younger women, to exhort "the young women to love their husbands, to love their children, to be sensible, pure, workers at home, kind, being subject to their own husbands, that the word of God may not be dishonored" (Titus 2:4-5). Older widows are to be enrolled in a special order in the church, apparently both to serve (cf. v. 13) and to receive care and remuneration; they are to be enrolled on the basis of their previous service in the church (I Tim. 5:9ff., esp. v. 10). But at the same time Paul opposes such an order for younger widows, preferring that they return to the condition which expresses their basic inclination and need—namely, the marital state and its privileges and responsibilities. (Men and women who do not have the inclination and need to be married—namely, those who have a gift from God to be single—he encourages to be single as an avenue of service but not as a condition for church office [cf. I Cor. 7]).

One of the most interesting references to women or wives in the midst of a discussion of church officers is the one in I Timothy 3:11 ("Women must likewise be dignified, not malicious gossips, but temperate, faithful in all things"). My opinion is that women are mentioned and their qualifications given in this passage because they are to be involved in the diaconal activities. They are not mentioned in the midst of the description of bishops because women are excluded from the ruling-teaching office. They are mentioned in the midst of the description of deacons because it is perfectly proper for them to be involved in the diaconal ministry, which does not involve inherently, ruling and teaching. It is also striking that the office of deacon is described not in both male and female terms or without any reference to sex, but in male terms, and the reference to women or wives appears in the midst of that description. It would seem therefore that the office of deacon is an office for men only, but that at the same time women are to be involved in that diaconal area. Therefore this writer would encourage churches to elect deaconesses who can help the deacons.

The significance of bishops and deacons being described as males may be challenged on the grounds that they also are described as being husbands and fathers. It could be insisted that if marriage and parenthood are not norms for officers (both bachelors and husbands without children are elected to such offices), then neither is maleness a norm. Here again Scripture must interpret Scripture. How does the church know that the apostle is describing officers in terms of the usual situation—marriage and a family—indicating that the way a man lives in that situation demonstrates his ability, and not mandating that officers be married and have children? It is possible that God would require such qualifications for office—compare some of the stringent requirements for office in the Old Testament! The answer is that the teaching of our Lord in Matthew 19:11-12 and the teaching of the apostle Paul in I Corinthians 7 (and his application of that teaching in I Corinthians 9:5 to himself as an apostle—an office which includes the concepts of elder or bishop [cf. I Peter 5:1; II John 1; III John 1]) indicates that marriage and children are not necessary for the officer. Why then does the apostle describe these offices in terms of married men with families? He does so because this was most commonplace for officers (cf. again I Cor. 9:5) and because a man's conduct in the marriage and family situation serves as one of the best indicators of his qualifications for office.

As for the offices being described in male terms, the case is otherwise. For one thing, women are prohibited in I Timothy 2:12 from teaching and ruling men. Furthermore the emphasis on man's headship in the home (I Tim. 3:4-5, 12) is correlated with man's responsibility and, in the case of the elder, with his authority in the church. This headship is a constant keynote in New Testament teaching on the role relationship of men and women and is constantly affirmed as the male responsibility. Finally women (or wives) are self-consciously mentioned and distinguished from the men and the offices mentioned (I Tim. 3:11). These considerations would seem to indicate that the male terminology is not in the same category as the marriage and family terminology. We may then draw the following conclusions: Scripture on the one hand shows the terms concerning marriage and the family to be relative, not absolute; on the other hand the terms concerning maleness are specifically supported and demanded in Scripture and are therefore not relative.

This leads us to consider Phoebe, the *diakonos* "of the church which is at Cenchrea" (Rom. 16:1–2). The first consideration is the meaning of *diakonos* at this place. This word is the common Greek word for servant (cf. John 2:5, 9). Christ is designated as a servant by this term (Rom. 15:8); the state is called a servant (Rom. 13:4); Christians are called servants of Christ and God (cf. John 12:26). And since the model for leadership in the church is the servant Jesus and since leadership is manifested in service, those leaders are called servants or ministers by means of this Greek word (cf. Matt. 20:26; Mark 10:43; I Cor. 3:5; II Cor. 3:6; 6:4; Eph. 3:7; 6:21; Col. 1:7, 23, 25; 4:7; I Thess. 3:2; I Tim. 4:6). Paul speaks of himself and others in these passages as servants or ministers of Christ, of God, and of the church. Finally the word is specially and specifically applied to those officers of the church whose task is primarily if not exclusively service—namely, the deacons, who bear this Greek word as their title, in distinction from the bishops (cf. Phil. 1:1; I Tim. 3:1, 8, 12).

The question is, In what sense is the term used in reference to Phoebe? The vast majority of modern English translations have not translated this term "minister" or "deacon" in reference to Phoebe, trying instead to express what they think Paul meant by the term. If the term is translated "minister" in reference to Paul and others as leaders of the church, and if Paul himself has ruled women out of the teaching-ruling offices, then it is appropriate to translate *diakonos* here as something other than "minister." Furthermore, in the passage where the term *diakonos* (translated "deacon") designates one special office, it is applied self-consciously to men but not to women (women are distinguished from deacons in this passage); out of regard for Paul's usage of this term, translators will not use the term "deacon" in reference to Phoebe the woman (cf. I Tim. 3:8ff., esp. v. 12). Phoebe, then, served in some very special and significant capacity of service in the church, but she was not a "deacon" in the official sense of the term.

Even if one were to translate *diakonos* in reference to Phoebe as "deacon," this would in no way overturn or alter the clear teaching of the apostle Paul in I Timothy 2:12 that a woman is not to teach or exercise authority over a man—that is, she is not to serve in ruling and teaching offices or functions. Theoretically one could ordain women to the office of deacon without directly challenging that Biblical teaching because the office of deacon involves service and not teaching or ruling per se.

The second consideration with reference to Phoebe is the meaning of *prostatis* in Romans 16:2: ". . . she herself has also been a helper [*prostatis*] of many, and of myself as well." The argument is that the word *prostatis* indicates that she was a ruler or had oversight in the church. It is true that the masculine form of this word *(prostatēs)* means "one who stands before, front-rank man, . . . leader, chief,"[29] but the feminine form, which is used here of Phoebe, means "protectress, patroness, helper."[30] So the argument turns more on the significance of the masculine form of the word than on the feminine form, which is the one used here. An analogy may help to show the danger of this kind of argument. The Greek word *presbyteros* in its masculine form can mean either "an older man" or "a leader in the church, an elder"; but the feminine form of the term, *presbytera*, certainly does not mean "church officer" or "elder" as well as "old woman"! (cf. I Tim. 5:2). Surely Jewett understands the term *prostatis* correctly when he says that its use in reference to Phoebe "should hardly be taken to mean that Phoebe was a woman 'ruler.' Rather the meaning would seem to be that she was one who cared

29. H. G. Liddell and Robert Scott, *A Greek-English Lexicon*, 9th ed. (New York: Oxford, 1940), p. 1526.

30. Bauer, Arndt, and Gingrich, *Greek-English Lexicon*, p. 726.

for the affairs of others by aiding them with her resources."[31]

Finally one turns to one of the most illustrious women in the New Testament church—Prisca (or Priscilla) the wife of Aquila (Acts 18:2, 18, 26; Rom. 16:3; I Cor. 16:19; II Tim. 4:19). Several things stand out about Prisca. She and her husband are named together, and her name is often first. Almost wherever they are, a church meets in their house (Rom. 16:5; I Cor. 16:19). They are both called Paul's "fellow-workers in Christ Jesus" (Rom. 16:3). And both of them take Apollos aside and explain to him "the way of God more accurately" (Acts 18:26). Full weight must be given to all that is said of her, and especially of whatever part she had in the personal and private ministry that she and Aquila exercised toward Apollos. But this personal and private ministry with her husband ("they," not "she," took Aquila aside) in no way negates the teaching of the New Testament that excludes a woman from a public ministry of teaching and ruling in the church (cf. again I Tim. 2:12).

Two facts emerge. The first is that none of the passages recognizing and encouraging women in their service in the church recognize or encourage them in the public and authoritative teaching-ruling offices or functions in reference to the church as a whole or to men in particular. The concrete data has reinforced, not minimized or refuted, that teaching. The second fact is that the New Testament and the apostles do recognize and encourage women to use their gifts in various other capacities in the life and service of the church. These two facts must be seen in correlation, and neither must be used to negate or overturn the other.

When one seeks to determine the areas and functions in which the gifts of women are utilized in the church, one finds that almost every area or function is in view except that which is specifically prohibited. Women pray and prophesy, and women perform various diaconal tasks and functions. The area of activity most often emphasized is that of diaconal service (cf. again I Tim. 3:11 in context;

31. *Man as Male and Female*, p. 170.

Rom. 16:1–2; I Tim. 5:10ff.). The writer would encourage churches to elect women to function as deaconesses, that is, to help the deacons. And even teaching and exercising authority are ruled out only when they involve the church as a whole or men in particular. Women are urged to teach other women in the church (Titus 2:3–5) and to exercise authority, under their husbands, over the household or home. (In I Timothy 5:14 "keep house" means literally, "manage one's household.") And it is evident that in a home where there is no father, the mother is the head. These considerations point up the fact that the Bible is saying or implying not that woman is inherently incapable of engaging in or exercising these gifts, but that God has ordained a role relationship between equals, men and women, in these areas of authority and leadership, giving to man the role of head in these areas.

Christians and churches faithful to Scripture and to the Creator-Redeemer who reveals His will in Scripture should encourage both the role relationship of men and women that God ordains and the free exercise, in harmony with the role relationship, of the gifts He gives both men and women.

4

Conclusion

Two General Objections

Two objections raised against the church's traditional view of the relationship of men and women relate to both marriage and the church, so we have waited until now to discuss them. One objection is of a philosophical nature, the other theological.

Paul K. Jewett and others insist that subordination (or submission) that rests on the fact of woman's femininity is intrinsically antithetical to equality and necessarily implies inferiority.[1]

But the New Testament insists, in opposition to Jewett, that subordination does not imply inferiority, even if the aspect of "ontology"—namely, femininity—is brought into the picture (cf. I Cor. 11:3). The apostle Paul in his appeal to the relation of God the Father to God the Son does not regard Christ's Sonship and resultant incarnation as implying His inferiority to the Father. Although Christ the Son's

---

1. *Man as Male and Female* (Grand Rapids: Eerdmans, 1975), p. 131.

submission is expressed in the areas of action and of incarnation (the areas of service and of the accomplishment of salvation; cf. also I Cor. 15:24–28), it is also an expression of the ontological relationship of preincarnate, submissive Sonship (cf., e.g., John 5:18–23, 30).

The ontological relationship analogous to that between man and woman, writes Paul, is that between Father and Son (I Cor. 11:3). That Christ submits as Son and as incarnate, i.e., because of certain ontological aspects, does not mean therefore that He is inferior to the Father, nor does it cast into doubt His deity. Likewise, that the woman submits as woman does not mean therefore that she is inferior or that her humanity as an image-bearer is threatened. In both cases, it is equals in relationship to one another. In both cases, one, because of His or her "ontological" and ordained role in relation to the other, acknowledges headship and submits. Just as no inferiority may be asserted or assumed for Christ in His submission, so also no inferiority may be asserted or assumed for woman, and no objection may be justly made because her submission rests on her cocreated identity as woman in relation to man.

The final objection we will discuss is this: In a most striking and vigorous way Jewett has said that some of Paul's teaching on this subject, including his exegesis of Genesis 2, reflects his rabbinic training and is wrong—that is, it is an erroneous human statement that should not be followed.[2]

The full impact of this evaluation must be reckoned with. It is saying that this portion of Scripture, the Word of God, is wrong in what it professes to teach. It is saying that not only the apostle Paul but also the apostle Peter are wrong. In fact, it is saying that all the instruction we get on the subject of marriage relative to this point, and on woman in authority in the church, in the whole New Testament and even in the whole Bible, is wrong. Let that come into focus. God has allowed His church, both in Old and New Testament days, and His apostles and writers to communicate on these subjects that which is

2. Ibid., pp. 134ff., 139, 145.

in error and out of accord with His revealed will. And not only that: we must say also that Jesus made no attempt to correct this misunderstanding in the areas of marriage and the church. In fact, by selecting twelve *men*, Jesus perpetuated this supposedly horrendous, male-chauvinist approach.

This view that the apostles taught error is maintained over against the apostles' assertion that what they taught is God's will and is founded on God's order. Paul asserts in I Timothy 2 that the exclusion of women from the ruling-teaching function of the church is based on the creation order, the most basic factor that touches all people everywhere. In I Corinthians 11 Paul appeals to the authority relationships that God has established between the Father and the Son, the Son and man, and man and woman (v. 3); this is the most comprehensive appeal to interpersonal relationships, involving even the relationship of the Son and the Father. And in I Corinthians 11:16 he affirms that this is the uniform view of the churches of God. In I Corinthians 14:34 he emphatically says that what he teaches is based on the law, another appeal to the creation order but now expressed by the term *law* as God's absolute standard. And finally, in reference to his teaching in I Corinthians 14—including that teaching on the subject under discussion—he says, "... the things which I write to you are the Lord's commandment" (v. 37)! The apostle Paul and also the apostle Peter insist the exact opposite of Jewett, and they are saying, "Thus says the Lord."

Notice finally that both the apostles and the church have realized that equality and differences of roles do indeed fit together, just as they have recognized that people are both equally image-bearers as men and women and also different as men and women. Must we view these two factors of equality and role differences as contradictory when they exist together in the creative activity of the Godhead and when both express God's will?

The Biblical Attitude

We must not conclude our discussion of this burning issue of the role relationship of men and women without also discussing the kind of attitudes and interpersonal relationships that must exist within the structure God has ordered. The Bible, as vigorously as it establishes order in civil government, the church, and the family, always joins to its statements about authority and submission, the keynote of right attitude. Once it has established the authority structure or pattern, it usually warns those in authority against misusing that authority (cf. elders in the church [I Peter 5:3] and fathers in the home [Eph. 6:4; Col. 3:21]). The same keynote must also be sounded in the role relationship that God has established between man and woman.

The backdrop for this affirmation is the corrosive effect of sin on interpersonal relationships in general and on that between a husband and wife in particular. It is noteworthy that Genesis 3 indicates that sin not only alienates human beings from God but also alienates men and women (Gen. 3:16). Sin accounts for much of the hostility and antagonism between the sexes now; men and women either misuse or rebel against their particular role in relation to one another in marriage and the church. The New Testament description of one's responsibilities and obligations in marriage takes this into account and stresses love, honor, and respect. Although the New Testament description of marriage affirms vigorously the husband-wife relationship as that of head and helper, it asks each partner to be what he or she is least likely to be (Eph. 5:22ff.; Col. 3:18–19; I Peter 3:1–7). To the husband as authority figure comes the vigorous admonition to love (as Christ loves the church), not to be bitter, and to honor his wife. To the wife as the under-authority figure comes the vigorous admonition to respect her husband and to submit ("as to the Lord" and as the church submits to Christ) "in everything." The tendency for the one in authority, affected by sin, is to be callous and overweening, disregarding the person and feelings of the one under his authority, but the New Testament requires just the opposite of husbands: ". . . live with your wives in an understanding way, as with a weaker vessel, since she is a woman; and grant her honor as a fellow-heir of the grace of life, so that your prayers may not be hindered" (I Peter 3:7). The tendency for one under authority, affected by sin, is to be sullen and disrespectful, complying as little as possible, but the New Testament requires just the opposite of the wife: "... let the wife see to it that she respect her husband" (Eph. 5:33; cf. 5:22–23; I Peter 3:4, 6).

But even these words and truths must be set in their wider context, and that context is the mutual submission that all Christians—men and women, husbands and wives— must render to each other under the headship of and in respect for the Lord Jesus Christ (Eph. 5:21: "... be subject to one another in the fear of Christ"; cf. I Cor. 11:11–12: "However, in the Lord, neither is woman independent of man, nor is man independent of woman"). The setting for all role relationships is that we all belong to, need, and must submit to one another as joint-heirs of the grace of life. Even in exercising his function as leader of others in the church, an elder or bishop must serve others. Even in exercising his headship over his wife, the husband must submit to and honor her as a joint-heir of the grace of life, an equal by both creation and redemption (again cf. I Peter 3:7). Elders and husbands are heads not because they are inherently superior—for they exercise their functions among and with equals—but because they have been called by God to their tasks.

It is this combined keynote of submission and equality in exercising leadership that I fear has been lost not only in the secular women's liberation movement but also on the part of the more strident voices within the Christian community. And to do so is to fall into the infighting for the places of honor and authority that the disciples of Jesus did (cf. Matt. 20:20 28 and parallels). (Parenthetically, Jesus' concept of servanthood renders groundless the charge that an appeal to submission is but an echo of authoritarianism and some more opiate for the people.) In His reply to His disciples, Jesus does not deny that some are called to positions of leadership; He does attempt to deal with the root sin of pride, arrogance, and self-righteousness. The model for all Christians, and especially for those in positions of leadership or headship, is Jesus Himself: "You know that the rulers of the Gentiles lord it over them, and their great men exercise authority over them. It is not so among you, but whoever wishes to become great among you shall be your servant, and whoever wishes to be first among you shall be your slave; just as the Son of Man did not come to be served, but to serve, and to give His life a ransom for many" (Matt. 20: 25-28).

The Christian church and individual Christians will most likely face in the coming day the charge that they are unrighteous and unjust in denying to women leadership roles in marriage and the church, or at least in not abolishing male leadership roles. We may well be maligned as unprincipled or prejudiced people, and we may suffer economic and legal sanctions. In such times when God's unchanging Word clashes with man's changing culture, let us fortify ourselves with the truth that

> *All flesh is like grass,*
> *And all its glory like the flower of grass.*
> *The grass withers,*
> *And the flower falls off,*
> *But the word of the Lord abides forever.*
> (I Peter 1:24-25)

Appendix:
Office in the New Testament
(and the Ministry of Women)

Author's note: The Reformed Ecumenical Synod, in January 1977, counted in its membership thirty-eight churches from Africa, Asia, Europe, North America, South America, and the South Pacific. Member churches in the United States are the Associate Reformed Presbyterian Church, the Christian Reformed Church of North America, the Orthodox Presbyterian Church, and the Reformed Presbyterian Church of North America (Covenanter). The "basis" of the RES *is the Scriptures, about which the Synod's constitution says, "... in their entirety as well as in every part thereof, [they] are the infallible and ever-abiding Word of the living Triune God absolutely authoritative in all matters of creed and conduct...." This paper was presented to the* RES *in 1972 by the Advisory Committee, and its recommendations were adopted in an amended form. It is here reprinted verbatim, except that the Scripture quotations have been changed from the American Standard Version to the New American Standard Bible, and that a few paragraphs have been omitted from section B, "Analysis."*

A. Materials

1. Report of Study Committee on "Office in the New Testament" (*Agenda, Reformed Ecumenical Synod: Australia 1972*, pp. 69–105).
2. Appendix or Minority Report of Study Committee (*Agenda*, pp. 134–35).
3. Contribution from J. Firet (*Agenda Supplement*, pp. 19–25).
4. Women and Ecclesiastical Offices, from Reformed Church of Argentina (*Agenda Supplement*, pp. 115–17).
5. Women and Office, from Christian Church of Sumba (*Agenda Supplement*, p. 18).
6. Ecclesiastical Office and Ordination, from Christian Reformed Church in the U.S.A. (*Agenda Supplement*, pp. 123, 127–28).

B. Analysis

"The study committee sought to carry out its assignment but at the same time indicated that the mandate cannot possibly be carried out literally by a study committee."[1] On the background of an in-depth study of the concept and nature of office in the Holy Scripture, the study committee gave particular attention to "the nature and essence of ordination and/or installation" in correlation with the New Testament expression of that activity by "a laying on of hands,"[2] and to the biblical teaching on "The Ministry of Women."[3] The study committee answered affirmatively to the question of the church of Brazil, whether an elder, in charge of the worship service, may pronounce the benediction. It argued that there is a unity of Word and sacrament and that therefore an elder gifted and called to minister the Word of God may also minister the benediction.[4]

1. "Report of Study Committee on 'Office in the New Testament,'" in *Agenda, Reformed Ecumenical Synod: Australia 1972*, p. 69.
2. Ibid., pp. 84–87.
3. Ibid., pp. 98–105.
4. Ibid., p. 87.

The Appendix (or Minority Report) differed from the committee report in emphasizing the relationship between "the seven" of Acts 6 and the deacons of I Timothy 3 and Philippians 1:1, in distinguishing the work of Philip and Stephen as evangelists (cf. Acts 21:8) from their work as "the seven," in considering the special function of the evangelist as continuing in the church today, and in maintaining that the laying on of hands is a uniform and normative practice in the New Testament for all offices and should be followed today. . . .

C. Observations

1. *Office.* The word *office* itself is not found in the New Testament, but the concept is found, for example, in the word *episkopē* (I Tim. 3:1) which may be rendered "office of bishop." More particularly, the Apostle Paul lists what may be designated as special offices in the church as gifts of Christ to the church (Eph. 4:11) and includes them among a wider list of *gifts* (charismata) (I Cor. 12:4ff.; cf. v. 28; less explicitly in Rom. 12:3–8). The diversities of gifts are also diversities of *services (diakonia)* (I Cor. 12:4; cf. v. 28) so that the words *service/servants (diakonia/diakonos)* become key words not only for the general office of believer but more particularly for special offices (for *diakonia* see Acts 1:25; 6:4; 12:25; 20:24; 21:19; Rom. 11:13; I Cor. 12:5; 16:15; II Cor. 4:1; 5:18; 6:3; 11:8; Col. 4:17; I Tim. 1:12; for *diakonos* see I Cor. 3:5; II Cor. 6:4; 11:23; Eph. 3:7; 6:21; Col. 1:7, 23, 25; 4:7; I Thess. 3:2; I Tim. 4:6; all on the background of Jesus' teaching in Matt. 20:25–28; Mark 10:42–45).

This concept of office, *service/servants,* covers a broad spectrum from the ministry of Paul the Apostle to that of fellow-workers such as Apollos and Timothy, and finally the term *diakonos* becomes a virtual technical term for that special office which is singularly involved in service, that of the *deacon* (I Tim. 3:8–13; Phil. 1:1).

2. *Bishops (elders) and deacons.* In the midst of a variety of terminology in reference to special gifts, offices, and services, a pattern does emerge of designating two

distinct special offices, those who rule and teach, and those who give aid and serve, or bishops and deacons (Phil. 1:1; I Tim. 3:1–13; cf. the latter with Acts 20:17 and 28, and Eph. 4:11). The distinction between these two offices is indicated by the qualifications and tasks required of each. The bishops (elders) are to rule and to teach (I Tim. 3:2, 5; 5:17; Titus 1:9ff.; Acts 20:28 and chapter 15; I Peter 5:1–4), the deacons are to serve (cf. Acts 6:2–3). This distinction is also manifest in their distinctive names, *bishops*, (*episkopos*, those who oversee others) and *deacons* (*diakonos*, those who serve others).

3. *Elders* (bishops). Certain significant truths appear when Scripture is compared with Scripture: (a) The rule or oversight is conducted by a plurality of elders in their corporate capacity and on a parity with one another. The reference to this office in terms of its existence in a church and its activity of ruling is always made in the plural (Acts 11:30; 14:23; chapter 15; 20:17, 28; Phil. 1:1; I Tim. 5:17; Titus 1:5; see also the Scripture under the following section [b]). (b) When it is taken into account that elders may be referred to by two titles (presbyters or bishops, Acts 20:17, 28; Titus 1:5, 7) or may be designated by their activity of ruling and teaching without any title, and when it is recognized therefore that this rule by elders is evident in virtually every area of the New Testament church and is referred to by virtually every New Testament author (Acts 11:30; 14:23; chapter 15; 20:17, 28; Phil. 1:1; I Thess. 5:12–13; I Tim. 3:1ff.; 5:17; Titus 1:5; Heb. 13:7, 17; James 5:14; I Peter 5:1ff.; cf. Rom. 12:7–8; I Cor. 12:28; 16:15; II John 1; III John 1) as well as being commanded by Paul (Titus 1:5), it becomes apparent that the government by elders is the one and normative pattern in the New Testament. (c) Within the unity of the one office of elder there are some "who work hard at preaching and teaching" (I Tim. 5:17). This has given rise to the designations "teaching elder" or "minister," and "ruling elder" or simply "elder."

4. *Laying on of hands* (ordination and/or installation). The advisory committee notes that elders (I Tim. 5:22) and "the seven" (Acts 6:6) as well as those commissioned

for special service (Acts 13:3) were appointed or set apart by the laying on of hands of all those who are included under the designation "presbytery" (*presbyterion,* I Tim. 4:14; cf. II Tim. 1:6; Acts 6:6; 13:3). The present difference in practice indicates that the various churches of the RES should study this question again and communicate their understanding of the New Testament practice and its significance.

5. *Ministry of women.* In view of the fact that the historic Christian and Reformed practice of limiting the office of ruling and preaching elders to men has been questioned by some churches in the RES[5] and that special attention has been given to this matter by the study committee report, the advisory committee would also give special attention to this in their observations so that it may be demonstrated "that it is the plain and obvious teaching of Scripture that women are excluded from the office of ruling and preaching elders." Two passages in the New Testament deal explicitly and directly with this subject in the context of the life of the church, I Timothy 2:11–15 and I Corinthians 14:33b–37. The Apostle, with his apostolic and thus normative authority, says specifically, "I do not allow a woman to teach or exercise authority over a man, but to remain quiet" (I Tim. 2:12). The prohibition is motivated within the statement itself by the fact that a woman must be in subjection to man (verse 11) and teaching and ruling or dominion over a man is a violation of this subjection. The reason for this prohibition is given in verses 13 and 14: "For it was Adam who was first created, and then Eve. And it was not Adam who was deceived, but the woman being quite deceived, fell into transgression." It may be summarized as the priority of Adam's (man's) creation to that of Eve (woman) and the fact of Eve's (woman's) being deceived or led astray. Paul thus appeals to the two great facts of God's significant order in creating man and woman and to the implications of the fall. The reference to the priority of Adam's creation

---

5. *Acts of Reformed Ecumenical Synod: Amsterdam 1968,* art. 84, p. 39, and items 3–5 of the materials.

to that of Eve refers to Genesis 2:18–25 with its teaching that the woman is created to assist man and be in subjection to him as the one who is the head over her (cf. I Cor. 11:2ff. and Eph. 5:22ff.). The significance of Eve's deception as a reason for the prohibition is not indicated here or elsewhere in the Scriptures. In the I Corinthians 14:33b–37 passage a similar prohibition is given, and there also reasons are given. The reasons are that women are to be in subjection "as the Law also says" (v. 34) and that "it is improper for a woman to speak in church" (v. 35). Here the Apostle indicates that God's law demands such subjection of women that they do not speak and teach in the church and that a violation of that demand of God's law is in itself shameful. Apparently the Corinthian church thought and practiced otherwise than Paul taught and apparently they had argued for a supposedly more liberated view of woman in the church (v. 36). Paul indicates that the command that women keep silence in the churches is to be observed in their church "as in all the churches of the saints" (v. 33b). Further, he rebukes their practice of letting women speak and teach contrary to the law of God and the practice in all the churches by asking in effect if only they have the word of God (v. 36). Finally, he concludes by indicating that this teaching about women not speaking and teaching in church is to be acknowledged by them and recognized as one of the things that "are the Lord's commandment" (v. 37). It should be carefully noted that these passages (I Tim. 2:11–15; I Cor. 14:33b–37) are not illustrations but commands, and that the reasons or grounds given are not time-bound, historically and culturally relative arguments that grow up out of or apply only to that day and age, but rather the way God created man and woman and the relationships God commanded that they should sustain to one another. When we realize that the office of ruling and preaching elders has as its essence the responsibility to teach in the church and to rule or have dominion in that church (see above), and that in reference to men also, we see that these commands of Paul exclude women from this office.

The fact that "there is neither male nor female, for you

are all one in Christ Jesus" (Gal. 3:28) does not deny the teaching of I Timothy 2 and I Corinthians 14 just as it does not deny man's maleness and woman's femaleness nor annul their relationship in the family (cf. Eph. 5:22ff.; for the significance of the correlation of man's rule in the family with his rule in the church, see I Timothy 3:4–5).

Even though I Timothy 2:11–15 and I Corinthians 14: 33b–37 exclude women from the teaching and ruling office in the church, other passages indicate that women are involved in diaconal tasks and even in appropriate teaching situations. A sampling of these activities may be seen in the following: older widows are enrolled by the church (I Tim. 5:9–16); older women are called upon to teach and train young women in reference to their responsibilities to their husbands and children (Titus 2:3–4); women (or wives, *gunaikas*) are referred to in the midst of the description of deacons (I Tim. 3:11); Phoebe is designated as "a servant [*diakonon*] of the church which is at Cenchrea" (Rom. 16:1); Paul referred to a situation in the Corinthian church where women are praying or prophesying (I Cor. 11:5); and Priscilla and Aquila, that inseparable wife-and-husband team, in a discreet and private meeting, expounded unto Apollos "the way of God more accurately" (Acts 18:26).

In considering the ministry of women in the church these three biblical truths must be held in correlation: (1) "There is neither male nor female; for you are all one in Christ Jesus" (Gal. 3:28); in their standing in and before Christ male and female are equal. (2) Women, by God's creative order, are to be in subjection to men in the home and church, and are therefore excluded from the office of ruling and preaching elders (Eph. 5:22; I Tim. 2:11–15; I Cor. 14:33b–37; cf. I Tim. 3:4–5). (3) Women have a unique function to fulfill in the diaconal task of the church and in appropriate teaching situations (cf., for example, I Tim. 3:11; 5:9ff.; Titus 2:3–4; Rom. 16:1).

D. Recommendations:

1. That Synod request the member churches to study further the biblical teaching concerning "the laying on

of hands" (ordination and/or installation) and present their finding to the next Synod of the RES. *Ground:* There is a divergence of understanding and practice among the churches and such re-evaluation of the Scriptures may hopefully bring the churches to a unified understanding and practice.

2. That Synod call the attention of the Reformed Church in Brazil to the argument and affirmative answer provided by the study committee to their question. *Ground:* The Reformed Church in Brazil has asked the RES for its advice and this is the answer the study committee has provided from their consideration of the Scriptures.

3. That Synod reaffirm that it is the teaching of Scripture that women are excluded from the office of ruling and preaching elders. *Ground:* The Scriptures indicate that for all the churches women are not permitted to teach nor to have dominion over men on the basis of God's order of creation, the implication of the fall, the explicit statement of the law, and the fact that the Apostle's command is itself "the commandment of the Lord" (I Tim. 2:11–15; I Cor. 14:33b–37).

4. That the Synod recommend to the member churches that because there is no clear Scriptural evidence for women occupying the office of deacons, they make full use of the gifts and services of women in the diaconal task in an auxiliary capacity and in appropriate teaching situations. *Ground:* Compare I Timothy 3:8–13 and the verses referred to above indicating the diaconal tasks and appropriate teaching situation of women.

GEORGE W. KNIGHT III
Reporter

General Index

Adam, 25, 31, 33, 40, 41, 42, 65
Adornment of good works, 30
Aischron, 37 n 14
Aland, Kurt, 45 n 20
Alexander, Ralph H., 35 n 13
American Lutherans, 16
Anēr, 30, 35 n 13
Angels, 34
Anthrōpos, 35 n 13
Apollos, 40, 52, 63, 67
Aquila, 40, 52, 67
Arndt, William F., 30 n 1, 30 n 3,
 31 n 4, 32 n 6, 33 n 7, 34 n 9,
 51 n 30
Associate Reformed Presbyterian
 Church, 61
Asthenēs, 20 n 1
Asthenesteroi skeuei, 20
Attitude(s), 57, 58
Authentein, 30
Authority, 9, 10, 24, 25, 26, 27,
 30, 31, 33, 35 n 13, 41, 42 n
 19, 43, 46, 49, 51, 53, 56, 57
 58, 59, 60

Balaam, 46
Bam, Brigalia, 16 n 9
Barrett, C. K., 30 n 2
Bartchy, S. Scott, 23 n 4
Bauer, Walter, 30 n 1, 30 n 3, 31
 n 4, 32 n 6, 33 n 7, 34 n 9, 51
 n 30
Bishops (or elders), 48, 49, 50,
 51, 58, 59, 62, 63 64, 67, 68
Bromiley, Geoffrey W., 20 n 1,
 33 n 6
Bruce, F. F., 34 n 11
Brunner, Peter, 16 n 6

Caesar, 24
Childbirth, 43, 44
Children and parents, 10, 14, 21–
 22, 23, 35
Christian Church of Sumba, 62
Christian Reformed Church of
 North America, 61, 62
Church life, 9, 16, 17, 18, 29, 37,
 39, 44, 45, 46, 47, 49, 51, 52,
 53, 55, 56, 57, 58, 59, 60, 66

Scripture Index

74

F
I

D

I